The Best IRC 199A Guide

The New 20% Business Income Deduction

CARTER MCBRIDE, JD

Copyright © 2018 Carter McBride

All rights reserved.

ISBN: 172713446X
ISBN-13: 978-1727134469

Table of Contents

I. Introduction
II. Definition of Key Terms
III. The Deduction in General
    A. Taxable Income below $157,500 ($315,000 MFJ)
        1. Computation with Capital Gains
        2. Wages from an S Corporation
        3. REIT and PTPs
    B. Taxable Income above $157,500 ($315,000 MFJ) – No SSTB
        1. Taxable Income below $207,500 ($415,000 MFJ)
        2. Phase-In Ranges (Taxable Income over $207,500 ($415,000 MFJ))
    C. SSTB
        1. Taxable Income below $207,500 ($415,000 MFJ)
        2. Taxable Income more than $207,500 ($415,000 MFJ)
IV. Trade or Business
    A. General Rules
    B. Self-Rentals
V. Qualified Business Income
    A. Defined
    B. Items Not Included in QBI
        1. Capital Gains and Losses, Including 1231 Gains and Losses
        2. Dividends
        3. Interest Income
        4. Gain or Loss from Transaction in Commodities or Excess Foreign Currency Gains
        5. Income from Notional Principal Contracts
        6. Annuities
        7. Qualified REIT Dividends and Qualified PTP Income
        8. Reasonable Compensation by an S Corporation Shareholder
        9. Guaranteed Payments to Partners
        10. 707(a) Payments Received by a Partner
    C. Disallowed Losses from Prior Years

      D. Net Operating Losses
      E. Clarification on Miscellaneous Rules
          1. IRC 481
          2. IRC 707(c)
          3. IRC 751
VI. W-2 Limitation
      A. General
      B. Third Party Payors
      C. W-2 Wages Defined
          1. Unmodified Box Method
          2. Modified Box Method
          3. Tracking Wages Method
          4. Short Tax Years
      D. Allocation of Wages to a Trade or Business and to QBI
          1. Trade or Business
          2. QBI
      E. Non-Duplication Rule
VII. UBIA
      A. General
      B. Specific Rules for Holding Periods
          1. Property Held for a Short Period
          2. Like-Kind Exchanges and Involuntary Conversions
          3. Tax Free Transactions
      C. Unadjusted Basis
      D. Allocating Basis in a RPE
          1. Partnerships
          2. S Corporations
VIII. SSTBs
      A. Heath
      B. Law
      C. Accounting
      D. Actuarial Science
      E. Performing Arts
      F. Consulting
      G. Athletics
      H. Financial Services
      I. Brokerage Services
      J. Investing and Investment Management
      K. Trading

- L. Dealing in Securities
- M. Dealing in Commodities
- N. Dealing in Partnership Interests
    - O. Any Trade or Business where the Reputation or Skill of the Employees or Owners is a Principal Asset
    - P. De Minimis Rule
    - Q. Anti-Abuse Rules
- IX. Loss Carryovers
- X. Aggregation
    - A. Aggregation – General Rule
    - B. Attribution
    - C. Election Statement
    - D. QBI Calculations with Aggregation
- XI. Miscellaneous Provisions
    - A. Basis in Partnership or S Corporation
    - B. Self-Employment Taxes
    - C. Net Investment Income Tax
    - D. Alternative Minimum Tax
    - E. Penalties
    - F. RPE Reporting Requirements

I. Introduction

Under the Tax Cuts and Jobs Act, Congress introduced a new tax deduction that is equal to 20 percent of a taxpayer's qualified business income under IRC 199A. This tax deduction raised many unanswered questions that taxpayers looked towards the IRS to answer.

The only current guidance taxpayers have is Regulation 1.199A-0 through 1.199A-6. The IRS also proposed Regulation 1.643(f)-1, which focuses on eliminating a technique of forming multiple trusts in order to circumvent any threshold limitations.

While at the time of this writing, the regulations are just proposed regulations, the IRS did include language in the regulations preamble that taxpayers can rely on these regulations for the 2018 tax year.

II. Definitions of Key Terms

Before jumping into the discussion of the new 20% deduction, a couple of terms needed to be defined, along with the acronyms practitioners are using:

Qualified Business Income (QBI) - for any taxable year, the net amount of qualified items of income, gain, deduction, and loss attributable to any qualified trade or business of the taxpayer.

Relevant Passthrough Entity (RPE) - a partnership (other than a PTP) or an S corporation that is owned, directly or indirectly by at least one individual, estate, or trust. A trust or estate is treated as an RPE to the extent it passes through QBI, W-2 wages, UBIA of qualified property, qualified REIT dividends, or qualified PTP income.

Specified Service Trade of Business (SSTB) - a specified service trade or business as defined in § 1.199A-5(b).

Unadjusted Basis Immediately After Acquisition (UBIA) - the basis on the placed in service date of the property as determined under section 1012 or other applicable sections of Chapter 1, including subchapters O (relating to gain or loss on dispositions of property), C (relating to corporate distributions and adjustments), K (relating to partners and partnerships), and P (relating to capital gains and losses).

III. The Deduction - In General

The general provision of IRC 199A states:

(a) In the case of a taxpayer other than a corporation, there shall be allowed as a deduction for any taxable year an amount equal to the sum of—

> **(1)** the lesser of—
>> **(A)** the combined qualified business income amount of the taxpayer, or
>> **(B)** an amount equal to 20 percent of the excess (if any) of—
>>> **(i)** the taxable income of the taxpayer for the taxable year, over
>>> **(ii)** the sum of any net capital gain (as defined in section 1(h)), plus the aggregate amount of the qualified cooperative dividends, of the taxpayer for the taxable year, plus
>
> **(2)** the lesser of—
>> **(A)** 20 percent of the aggregate amount of the qualified cooperative dividends of the taxpayer for the taxable year, or
>> **(B)** taxable income (reduced by the net capital gain (as so defined)) of the taxpayer for the taxable year.

The amount determined under the preceding sentence shall not exceed the taxable income (reduced by the net capital gain (as so defined)) of the taxpayer for the taxable year.

Breaking this down, taxpayers will be allowed a deduction equal to either 1) the combined potential qualified business income deduction amount or 2) an amount equal to 20 percent of the excess of taxable income over the sum of any net capital gain plus qualified cooperative dividends.

A. Taxable Income below $157,500 ($315,000 Married Filing Jointly)

The easiest calculation occurs when the taxpayer's taxable income is below $157,500 (or $315,000 Married Filing Jointly, MFJ). When below these threshold amounts, taxpayers do not need to worry about being an SSTB or not or any of the more complex calculations involved with this deduction. The calculation is purely 20% of QBI limited to 20% of total taxable income.

Example

> A, an unmarried individual, owns and operates a computer repair shop as a sole proprietorship. The business generated $100,000 in net taxable income from operations in 2018. A has no capital gains or losses. After allowable deductions not relating to the business, A's total taxable income for 2018 is $81,000. The business's QBI is $100,000, the net amount of its qualified items of income, gain, deduction, and loss. A's section 199A deduction for 2018 is equal to $16,200, the lesser of 20% of A's QBI from the business ($100,000 × 20% = $20,000) and 20% of A's total taxable income for the taxable year ($81,000 × 20% = $16,200).

1. Computation with Capital Gains

The example becomes a little more complicated when factoring in capital gains. Capital gains require you to decrease taxable income by the amount net capital gains.

Example

Assume the same facts as in Example 1 of this paragraph (c)(3), except that A also has $7,000 in net capital gain for 2018 and that, after allowable deductions not relating to the business, A's taxable income for 2018 is $74,000. A's taxable income minus net capital gain is $67,000 ($74,000–$7,000). A's section 199A deduction is equal to $13,400, the lesser of 20% of A's QBI from the business ($100,000 × 20% = $20,000) and 20% of A's total taxable income minus net capital gain for the taxable year ($67,000 × 20% = $13,400).

2. Wages from an S Corporation

With S Corporations, QBI is determined at the S Corporation level. Officer wages are a qualified item of deduction when calculating QBI.

Example

B and C are married and file a joint individual income tax return. B earned $500,000 in wages as an employee of an unrelated company in 2018. C owns 100% of the shares of X, an S corporation that provides landscaping services. X generated $100,000 in net income from operations in 2018. X paid C $150,000 in wages in 2018. B and C have no capital gains or losses. After allowable deductions not related to X, B and C's total taxable income for 2018 is $270,000. B's and C's wages are not considered to be income from a trade or business for purposes of the section 199A deduction. Because X is an S corporation, its QBI is determined at the S corporation level. X's QBI is $100,000, the net amount of its qualified items of income, gain, deduction, and loss. The wages paid by X to C are considered to be a qualified item of deduction for purposes of determining X's QBI. The section 199A deduction with respect to X's QBI is then determined by C, X's sole shareholder, and is claimed on the joint return filed by B and C. B and C's section 199A deduction is equal to $20,000, the lesser of 20% of C's QBI from the business

($100,000 × 20% = $20,000) and 20% of B and C's total taxable income for the taxable year ($270,000 × 20% = $54,000).

3. REIT and PTPs

Qualified REITs and Qualified PTPs are also able to receive the 20 percent tax deduction as well. These are calculated apart from regular QBI.

Example

Assume the same facts as the previous example except that B also earns $1,000 in qualified REIT dividends and $500 in qualified PTP income in 2018, increasing taxable income to $271,500. B and C's section 199A deduction is equal to $20,300, the lesser of (i) 20% of C's QBI from the business ($100,000 × 20% = $20,000) plus 20% of B's combined qualified REIT dividends and qualified PTP income ($1,500 × 20% = $300) and (ii) 20% of B and C's total taxable for the taxable year ($271,500 × 20% = $54,300).

B. Taxable Income above $157,500 ($315,000 Married Filing Jointly) – No SSTB

When taxable income is above $157,500 ($315,000 married filing jointly) and the taxpayer is not involved in an SSTB, we need to look if taxable income is also above or below $207,500 ($415,000 married filing jointly).

1. Taxable Income below $207,500 ($415,000 Married Filing Jointly)

If taxable income is above $157,500 ($315,000 Married Filing Jointly), but below $207,500 ($415,000 married filing jointly) and the taxpayer does not have an SSTB, the first part of the calculation is to apply the wage limitation:

Wage Limitation Calculation

Step 1 – Calculate 20% of QBI
Step 2 – Calculate 50% of Qualified W-2 Wages
Step 3 – Calculate 25% of Qualified W-2 Wages + 2.5% of UBIA
Step 4 – Take the Greater of Steps 2 and 3
Step 5 – Take the Lesser of Step 1 and 4

Example

> D, an unmarried individual, owns several parcels of land that D manages and which are leased to several suburban airports for parking lots. The business generated $1,000,000 of QBI in 2018. The business paid no wages and the property was not qualified property because it was not depreciable. After allowable deductions unrelated to the business, D's total taxable income for 2018 is $980,000. Because D's taxable income exceeds the applicable threshold amount, D's section 199A deduction is subject to the W-2 wage and UBIA of qualified property limitations. D's section 199A deduction is limited to zero because the business paid no wages and held no qualified property.

Applying the wage limitation calculation to this example:

Step 1 – Calculate 20% of QBI ($1,000,000 * 20% = $200,000)
Step 2 – Calculate 50% of Qualified W-2 Wages ($0)
Step 3 – Calculate 25% of Qualified W-2 Wages + 2.5% of UBIA ($0)
Step 4 – Take the Greater of Steps 2 and 3 ($0)
Step 5 – Take the Lesser of Step 1 and 4 ($0)

Since the result is $0, then the deduction is equal to $0.

The next example covers a non-SSTB that pays no wages, but does have UBIA.

Example

> Assume the same facts as in Example 1 of this paragraph (d)(4), except that D developed the land parcels in 2019,

expending a total of $10,000,000 to build parking structures on each of the parcels, all of which is depreciable. During 2020, D leased the parking structures and the land to the suburban airports. D reports $4,000,000 of QBI for 2020. After allowable deductions unrelated to the business, D's total taxable income for 2020 is $3,980,000. Because D's taxable income is above the threshold amount, the QBI component of D's section 199A deduction is subject to the W-2 wage and UBIA of qualified property limitations. Because the business has no W-2 wages, the QBI component of D's section 199A deduction will be limited to the lesser of 20% of the business's QBI or 2.5% of its UBIA of qualified property.

Twenty percent of the $4,000,000 of QBI is $800,000. Two and one-half percent of the $10,000,000 UBIA of qualified property is $250,000. The QBI component of D's section 199A deduction is thus limited to $250,000. D's section 199A deduction is equal to the lesser of (i) 20% of the QBI from the business as limited ($250,000) or (ii) 20% of D's taxable income ($3,980,000 × 20% = $796,000). Therefore, D's section 199A deduction for 2020 is $250,000.

Applying the wage limitation to this example:

Step 1 – Calculate 20% of QBI ($4,000,000 * 20% = $800,000)
Step 2 – Calculate 50% of Qualified W-2 Wages ($0)
Step 3 – Calculate 25% of Qualified W-2 Wages + 2.5% of UBIA ($10,000,000 * 2.5% = $250,000)
Step 4 – Take the Greater of Steps 2 and 3 ($250,000)
Step 5 – Take the Lesser of Step 1 and 4 ($250,000)

Since the result is above $0, multiply taxable income by 20% ($3,980,000 * 20% = $796,000). Step 4 was $250,000, which is less than the $796,000, so the deduction is $250,000.

The next example covers a non-SSTB that pays wages and has UBIA.

Example

E, an unmarried individual, is a 30% owner of LLC, which is classified as a partnership for Federal income tax purposes. In 2018, the LLC has a single trade or business and reported QBI of $3,000,000. The LLC paid total W-2 wages of $1,000,000, and its total UBIA of qualified property is $100,000. E is allocated 30% of all items of the partnership. For the 2018 taxable year, E reports $900,000 of QBI from the LLC. After allowable deductions unrelated to LLC, E's taxable income is $880,000. Because E's taxable income is above the threshold amount, the QBI component of E's section 199A deduction will be limited to the lesser of 20% of E's share of LLC's QBI or the greater of the W-2 wage or UBIA of qualified property limitations.

Twenty percent of E's share of QBI of $900,000 is $180,000. The W-2 wage limitation equals 50% of E's share of the LLC's wages ($300,000) or $150,000. The UBIA of qualified property limitation equals $75,750, the sum of 25% of E's share of LLC's wages ($300,000) or $75,000 plus 2.5% of E's share of UBIA of qualified property ($30,000) or $750. The greater of the limitation amounts ($150,000 and $75,750) is $150,000. The QBI component of E's section 199A deduction is thus limited to $150,000, the lesser of 20% of QBI ($180,000) and the greater of the limitations amounts ($150,000). E's section 199A deduction is equal to the lesser of 20% of the QBI from the business as limited ($150,000) or 20% of E's taxable income ($880,000 × 20% = $176,000). Therefore, E's section 199A deduction is $150,000 for 2018.

Applying the steps to this example:

Step 1 – Calculate 20% of QBI ($900,000 * 20% = $180,000)
Step 2 – Calculate 50% of Qualified W-2 Wages ($300,000 * 50% = $150,000)
Step 3 – Calculate 25% of Qualified W-2 Wages + 2.5% of UBIA ($300,000 * 25% + $30,000 * 2.5% = $75,750)

Step 4 – Take the Greater of Steps 2 and 3 ($150,000)
Step 5 – Take the Lesser of Step 1 and 4 ($150,000)

20% of E's taxable income is $176,000 ($880,000 × 20% = $176,000), so the deduction is allowed at $150,000.

2. Phase-In Ranges (Taxable Income over $207,500 ($415,000 Married Filing Jointly)

If taxable income is more than $207,500 ($415,000 for Married Filing Jointly) a phase-in calculation needs to occur.

After the first four steps, we need to change step 5 to:

Step 5: Is Step 4 Greater than Step 1?

If Step 4 is greater than Step 1, then use the amount from Step 1 as the QBI deduction. If Step 4 is less than Step 1, then we need to calculate Applicable Percentage:

Applicable Percentage Calculation
Step 6 – Subtract the threshold amount from taxable income, then divide by $50,000 ($100,000 for MFJ)
Step 7 – Subtract Step 4 from Step 1 and multiply by the amount in Step 6.
Step 8 – Subtract Step 7 from Step 1.

Example

(i) B and C are married and file a joint individual income tax return. B is a shareholder in M, an entity taxed as an S corporation for Federal income tax purposes that conducts a single trade or business. M holds no qualified property. B's share of the M's QBI is $300,000 in 2018. B's share of the W-2 wages from M in 2018 is $40,000. C earns wage income from employment by an unrelated company. After allowable deductions unrelated to M, B and C's taxable income for 2018 is $375,000. B and C are within the phase-in range because their taxable income exceeds the applicable threshold amount, $315,000, but does not exceed the threshold amount plus $100,000, or $415,000. Consequently, the QBI component of B and C's section 199A deduction may be limited by the W-2 wage and UBIA of qualified property limitations but the limitations will be phased in.

Here, their taxable income is $375,000, so it is between $315,000 and $415,000. This means the phase in calculation is required.

> The UBIA of qualified property limitation amount is zero because M does not hold qualified property. B and C must apply the W-2 wage limitation by first determining 20% of B's share of M's QBI. Twenty percent of B's share of M's QBI of $300,000 is Start Printed Page 40914$60,000. Next, B and C must determine 50% of B's share of M's W-2 wages. Fifty percent of B's share of M's W-2 wages of $40,000 is $20,000. Because 50% of B's share of M's W-2 wages ($20,000) is less than 20% of B's share of M's QBI ($60,000), B and C must determine the QBI component of their section 199A deduction by reducing 20% of B's share of M's QBI by the reduction amount.

The phase-in calculation is the calculated as:

> B and C are 60% through the phase-in range (that is, their taxable income exceeds the threshold amount by $60,000 and their phase-in range is $100,000). B and C must determine the excess amount, which is the excess of 20% of B's share of M's QBI, or $60,000, over 50% of B's share of M's W-2 wages, or $20,000. Thus, the excess amount is $40,000. The reduction amount is equal to 60% of the excess amount, or $24,000. Thus, the QBI component of B and C's section 199A deduction is equal to $36,000, 20% of B's $300,000 share M's QBI (that is, $60,000), reduced by $24,000. B and C's section 199A deduction is equal to the lesser of 20% of the QBI from the business as limited ($36,000) or (ii) 20% of B and C's taxable income

($375,000 × 20% = $75,000). Therefore, B and C's section 199A deduction is $36,000 for 2018.

Applying the applicable percentage calculation:

Already calculated:
Step 1 - $60,000
Step 4 - $20,000

Step 6 – Subtract the threshold amount from taxable income, then divide by $50,000 ($100,000 for MFJ) - $375,000 - $315,000 = $60,000 / $100,000 = 60%.
Step 7 – Subtract Step 4 from Step 1 and multiply by the amount in Step 6. - $60,000 - $20,000 = $40,000 * 60% = $24,000.
Step 8 – Subtract Step 7 from Step 1 - $60,000 – 24,000 = $36,000

20% of C's taxable income is $75,000 ($375,000 × 20% = $75,000) so the deduction is $36,000.

C. SSTB

When calculating the deduction for an SSTB, we need to first look at the total taxable income. Remember, if taxable income is below $157,500 ($315,000 for married filing jointly) then it does not matter if the business is an SSTB. If taxable income is less than $207,500 ($415,000 married filing jointly, then we need to limit the deduction. If taxable income is more than $207,500 ($415,000 married filing jointly) then no tax deduction is allowed.

1. Taxable Income Less than $207,500 ($415,000 MFJ)

If taxable income is less than $207,500 ($415,000 for MFJ), we need to follow these steps in order to calculate the potential QBI deduction:

Step 1 – Calculate 20% of QBI
Step 2 – Calculate 50% of Qualified W-2 Wages
Step 3 – Calculate 25% of Qualified Q-2 Wages + 2.5% UBIA

Step 4 – Take Greater of Step 2 and 3
Step 5 – Subtract the threshold amount from taxable income, then divide by $50,000 ($100,000 MFH)
Step 6 – Calculate 100% minus Step 5
Step 7 – Take Lesser of Step 1 and Step 4
Step 8 – Multiply Step 6 by Step 7

Example

B and C are married and file a joint individual income tax return. B is a shareholder in M, an entity taxed as an S corporation for Federal income tax purposes that conducts a single trade or business that is an SSTB. M holds no qualified property. B's share of the M's QBI is $300,000 in 2018. B's share of the W-2 wages from M in 2018 is $40,000. C earns wage income from employment by an unrelated company. After allowable deductions unrelated to M, B and C's taxable income for 2018 is $375,000. B and C are within the phase-in range because their taxable income exceeds the applicable threshold amount, $315,000, but does not exceed the threshold amount plus $100,000, or $415,000. Consequently, the QBI component of B and C's section 199A deduction may be limited by the W-2 wage and UBIA of qualified property limitations but the limitations will be phased in.

Because B and C are within the phase-in range, B must reduce the QBI and W-2 wages allocable to B from M to the applicable percentage of those items. B and C's applicable percentage is 100% reduced by the percentage equal to the ratio that their taxable income for the taxable year ($375,000) exceeds their threshold amount ($315,000), or $60,000, bears to $100,000. Their applicable percentage is 40%. The applicable percentage of B's QBI is ($300,000 × 40% =) $120,000, and the applicable percentage of B's share of W-2 wages is ($40,000 × 40% =) $16,000. These reduced numbers must then be used to determine how B's section 199A deduction is limited.

B and C must apply the W-2 wage limitation by first determining 20% of B's share of M's QBI as limited by paragraph (i) of this example. Twenty percent of B's share of M's QBI of $120,000 is $24,000. Next, B and C must determine 50% of B's share of M's W-2 wages. Fifty percent of B's share of M's W-2 wages of $16,000 is $8,000. Because 50% of B's share of M's W-2 wages ($8,000) is less than 20% of B's share of M's QBI ($24,000), B and C's must determine the QBI component of their section 199A deduction by reducing 20% of B's share of M's QBI by the reduction amount.

B and C are 60% through the phase-in range (that is, their taxable income exceeds the threshold amount by $60,000 and their phase-in range is $100,000). B and C must determine the excess amount, which is the excess of 20% of B's share of M's QBI, as adjusted in paragraph (i) of this example or $24,000, over 50% of B's share of M's W-2 wages, as adjusted in paragraph (i) of this example, or $8,000. Thus, the excess amount is $16,000. The reduction amount is equal to 60% of the excess amount or $9,600. Thus, the QBI component of B and C's section 199A deduction is equal to $14,400, 20% of B's share M's QBI of $24,000, reduced by $9,600. B and C's section 199A deduction is equal to the lesser of 20% of the QBI from the business as limited ($14,400) or 20% of B's and C's taxable income ($375,000 × 20% = $75,000). Therefore, B and C's section 199A deduction is $14,400 for 2018.

2. **Taxable Income more than $207,500 ($415,000 Married Filing Jointly)**

No deduction is allowed is a taxpayer has an SSTB and his taxable income is over $207,500 ($415,000 married filing jointly).

Example

Individual A has a solo practice accounting firm and files single. In tax year 2018, his taxable income was $300,000 and his QBI was a $200,000. No IRC 199A deduction is allowed as his taxable income is more than $207,500.

IV. Trade or Business

Now that the basic outline of the calculating the deduction is laid out, it is time to take a closer look at some of the finer details of the deduction.

A. General Rules

The first issue is what exactly is a trade or business under IRC 199A? Reg 1.199A-1(b) provides us the definition as:

> Trade or business means a section 162 trade or business other than the trade or business of performing services as an employee. In addition, rental or licensing of tangible or intangible property (rental activity) that does not rise to the level of a section 162 trade or business is nevertheless treated as a trade or business for purposes of section 199A, if the property is rented or licensed to a trade or business which is commonly controlled under § 1.199A-4(b)(1)(i) (regardless of whether the rental activity and the trade or business are otherwise eligible to be aggregated under § 1.199A-4(b)(1)).

This definition provides us an answer to one common question, will rental activities be subject to IRC 199A. Unfortunately, they will not unless they rise to the level of an IRC 162 trade or business.

B. Self-Rentals

The Regulation the directly addresses the issue of self-rentals:

> The proposed regulations extend the definition of trade or business for purposes of section 199A beyond section 162 in one circumstance. Solely for purposes of section 199A, the rental or licensing of tangible or intangible property to a

related trade or business is treated as a trade or business if the rental or licensing and the other trade or business are commonly controlled under proposed § 1.199A-4(b)(1)(i). It is not uncommon that for legal or other non-tax reasons taxpayers may segregate rental property from operating businesses. This rule allows taxpayers to aggregate their trades or businesses with the associated rental or intangible property under proposed § 1.199A-4 if all of the requirements of proposed § 1.199A-4 are met. In addition, this rule may prevent taxpayers from improperly allocating losses or deductions away from trades or businesses that generate income that is eligible for a section 199A deduction.

Only commonly controlled self-rentals do not need to rise to the level of an IRC 162 trade or business.

Common control is defined as:

> The same person or group of persons, directly or indirectly, owns 50 percent or more of each trade or business to be aggregated, meaning in the case of such trades or businesses owned by an S corporation, 50 percent or more of the issued and outstanding shares of the corporation, or, in the case of such trades or businesses owned by a partnership, 50 percent or more of the capital or profits in the partnership;

Example

S Corporation A is an IRC 162 trade or business owned by Amy and Bill, 50-50. Amy and Bill also own Building A, LLC 50-50. Building A is rented to S Corporation A as a self-rental but does not rise to an IRC 162 trade or business. Under Reg. 1.199A-4(b)(1)(i), there is common control and Building A is a considered a trade or business.

V. Qualified Business Income

A. Defined

QBI is defined as, for any taxable year, the net amount of qualified items of income, gain, deduction, and loss attributable to any qualified trade or business of the taxpayer. QBI does not include any qualified REIT dividends or qualified PTP income. Section 199A(c)(3)(A) provides that the term "qualified items of income, gain, deduction, and loss" means items of income, gain, deduction, and loss to the extent such items are (i) effectively connected with the conduct of a trade or business within the United States (within the meaning of section 864(c), determined by substituting "qualified trade or business (within the meaning of section 199A)" for "nonresident alien individual or a foreign corporation" or for "a foreign corporation" each place it appears), and (ii) included or allowed in determining taxable income for the taxable year.

B. Items Not Included In QBI

Several items need to be subtracted out of the QBI calculation.

1. Capital Gains and Losses, Including 1231 Gains and Losses

Short-term and long-term capital gains and losses are excluded from QBI. Under Section 1231, there is the possibility for capital or ordinary treatment of gains or losses. If Section 1231 creates a capital gain or loss, then these amounts are not added to QBI. If Section1 231 creates an ordinary gain or loss, then these amounts are added to QBI.

2. Dividends

Any income that is a dividend, is an equivalent of a dividend, and any payment in lieu of a dividend under IRC 954(c)(1)(G) is not added to QBI.

3. Interest Income

Only interest income allocable to a trade or business is allowed to count towards QBI. All other interest income is not counted for the purposes of QBI.

4. Gain or Loss from Transaction in Commodities or Excess Foreign Currency Gains

Any gain or loss from a transaction in commodities or excess foreign currency gains are not considered QBI.

5. Income from Notional Principal Contracts

Notional principal contracts are not considered QBI.

6. Annuities

Annuities are not considered QBI unless they are received as income in connection with a trade or business.

7. Qualified REIT Dividends and Qualified PTP Income

Qualified REIT dividends and qualified PTI income will not count as QBI but have a separate calculation.

Qualified REIT dividends are any dividend from a REIT received during the taxable year which:

Is not a capital gain dividend, as defined in section 857(b)(3), and

Is not qualified dividend income, as defined in section 1(h)(11).

A REIT dividend is not a qualified REIT dividend if the stock with respect to which it is received is held for fewer than 45 days, taking into account the principles of section 246(c)(3) and (4).

Qualified PTP income means the sum of:

> The net amount of such taxpayer's allocable share of income, gain, deduction, and loss from a PTP as defined in section 7704(b) that is not taxed as a corporation under section 7704(a), plus
>
> Any gain or loss attributable to assets of the PTP giving rise to ordinary income under section 751(a) or (b) that is considered attributable to the trades or businesses conducted by the partnership.

8. Reasonable Compensation by an S Corporation Shareholder

Reasonable compensation only applies to S Corporations for IRC 199A. Reasonable compensation by an S Corporation shareholder is deducted from QBI but it is not added back to QBI.

The reasonable compensation is not allowed to generate additional QBI deduction.

9. Guaranteed Payments to a Partner

Guaranteed payments to a partner are not considered QBI income, but if connected to the business, they could be a deduction from QBI.

Guaranteed payments under this section include guaranteed payments to non-individual partners as well.

10. 707(a) Payments Received by a Partner

The regulations eliminate all IRC 707(a) payments from QBI.

C. Disallowed Losses from Prior Years

Generally, previously disallowed losses or deductions (including under sections 465, 469, 704(d), and 1366(d)) allowed in the taxable year are taken into account for purposes of computing QBI. However, losses or deductions that were disallowed, suspended, limited, or carried over from taxable years ending before January 1, 2018 (including under sections 465, 469, 704(d), and 1366(d)), are not taken into account in a later taxable year for purposes of computing QBI.

D. Net Operating Losses

Net operating losses carried forward to future years are not taken into account when calculating QBI.

Under IRC 461(f), non-corporate taxpayers cannot claim more than $250,000 ($500,000 for married filing jointly) net business losses. Any losses above those amounts are carried forward to future years. Since these amounts were never taken into account for calculating QBI in the year that it arose, then the future year losses will be taken into account when calculating QBI in future years.

E. Clarification on Miscellaneous Rules

The IRS clarified several other issues in their regulations to IRC 199A.

1. IRC 481

IRC 481(a) adjustments, both positive and negative, are considered for QBI if the adjustment occurs in taxable years after December 31, 2017.

2. IRC 707(c)

If a partnership makes a guaranteed payment to a partner in exchange for the use of capital under IRC 707(c), the payments are not considered attributable to a trade or business, and thus do not constitute QBI. However, the partnership's related expense for making the guaranteed payments may constitute QBI if the other requirements are satisfied

3. IRC 751

Section 751 gains and losses on hot assets is considered QBI.

VI. W-2 Limitation

A. General

Depending on the taxpayer's taxable income, the W-2 wage limitation may apply. The regulations provide a three step method to allocate W-2 wages to a trade or business.

Step 1 – Determine W-2 wages based on Reg. 1.199A-2(b)(3)

Step 2 – Allocate W-2 wages between trades or businesses as laid out in Reg. 1.199A-2(b)(3); and

Step 3 – Determine W-2 wages allocable to QBI per Reg 1.199A-2(b)(4).

Wages only include wages from corporate officers and common law employees.

Statutory employees' wages paid are not considered for this calculation.

Forms W-2 must be filed with Social Security Administration within 60 days after their due date. If filed after 60 days, the taxpayer cannot use the W-2 wages as part of the calculation.

B. Third Party Payors

Businesses can include wages paid by third party payors.

> Specifically, the proposed regulations provide that, in determining W-2 wages, a person may take into account any W-2 wages paid by another person and reported by the other person on Forms W-2 with the other person as the

employer listed in Box c of the Forms W-2, provided that the W-2 wages were paid to common law employees or officers of the person for employment by the person. In such cases, the person paying the W-2 wages and reporting the W-2 wages on Forms W-2 is precluded from taking into account such wages for purposes of determining W-2 wages with respect to that person. Persons that pay and report W-2 wages on behalf of or with respect to others can include certified professional employer organizations under section 7705, statutory employers under section 3401(d)(1), and agents under section 3504. Under this rule, persons who otherwise qualify for the deduction under section 199A are not limited in applying the deduction merely because they use a third party payor to pay and report wages to their employees

C. W-2 Wages Defined

The IRS provided three methods for calculating W-2 Wages:

1. Unmodified Box Method
2. Modified Box 1 Method
3. Tracking Wages Method

1. Unmodified Box Method

Under the unmodified box method, W-2 wages are calculated by taking, without modification, the lesser of:

> The total entries in Box 1 of all Forms W-2 filed with SSA by the taxpayer with respect to employees of the taxpayer for employment by the taxpayer; or

> The total entries in Box 5 of all Forms W-2 filed with SSA by the taxpayer with respect to employees of the taxpayer for employment by the taxpayer.

This is easiest way to make the calculation, but will not always be the most accurate method.

2. Modified Box 1 Method

W-2 wages under this method are calculated as follows:

> Total the amounts in Box 1 of all Forms W-2 filed with SSA by the taxpayer with respect to employees of the taxpayer for employment by the taxpayer;
>
> Subtract from the total above amounts included in Box 1 of Forms W-2 that are not wages for Federal income tax withholding purposes, including amounts that are treated as wages for purposes of income tax withholding under section 3402(o) (for example, supplemental unemployment compensation benefits within the meaning of Rev. Rul. 90-72); and
>
> Add the total of the amounts that are reported in Box 12 of Forms W-2 with respect to employees of the taxpayer for employment by the taxpayer and that are properly coded D, E, F, G, and S.

3. Tracking Wages Methods

W-2 wages under this method are calculated as follows:

> Total the amounts of wages subject to Federal income tax withholding that are paid to employees of the taxpayer for employment by the taxpayer and that are reported on Forms W-2 filed with SSA by the taxpayer for the calendar year; and
>
> Add the total of the amounts that are reported in Box 12 of Forms W-2 with respect to employees of the taxpayer for employment by the taxpayer and that are properly coded D, E, F, G, and S.

4. Short Tax Years

The W-2 wages of the taxpayer for the short taxable year shall include only those wages paid during the short taxable year to employees of the taxpayer, only those elective deferrals (within the meaning of section 402(g)(3)) made during the short taxable year by employees of the taxpayer, and only compensation actually deferred under section 457 during the short taxable year with respect to employees of the taxpayer.

During a short taxable year, the taxpayer must use the tracking wages method. These are calculated as:

> The total amount of wages subject to Federal income tax withholding and reported on Form W-2 must include only those wages subject to Federal income tax withholding that are actually or constructively paid to employees during the short taxable year and reported on Form W-2 for the calendar year ending with or within that short taxable year (or, for a short taxable year that does not contain a calendar year ending with or within such short taxable year, wages subject to Federal income tax withholding that are actually or constructively paid to employees during the short taxable year and reported on Form W-2 for the calendar year containing such short taxable year); and

> For purposes of section 5.03(B), only the portion of the total amounts reported in Box 12, Codes D, E, F, G, and S on Forms W-2, that are actually deferred or contributed during the short taxable year are included in W-2 wages.

D. Allocation of Wages to a Trade or Business and to QBI

1. Trade or Business

If an individual or an RPE directly conducts multiple trades or businesses, and has items of QBI which are properly attributable to more than one trade or business, the individual or RPE must allocate those items among the several trades or businesses to which they are attributable using a reasonable method based on all the facts and circumstances. The individual or RPE may use a different reasonable method for different items of income, gain, deduction, and loss. The chosen reasonable method for each item must be consistently applied from one taxable year to another and must clearly reflect the income and expenses of each trade or business. The overall combination of methods must also be reasonable based on all facts and circumstances. The books and records maintained for a trade or business must be consistent with any allocations under this paragraph.

2. QBI

Once W-2 wages for each trade or business have been determined, each individual or RPE must identify the amount of W-2 wages properly allocable to QBI for each trade or business. W-2 wages are properly allocable to QBI if the associated wage expense is taken into account in computing QBI under §1.199A-3. In the case of an RPE, the wage expense must be allocated and reported to the partners or shareholders of the RPE as required by the Code, including subchapters K and S. The RPE must also identify and report the associated W-2 wages to its partners or shareholders.

E. Non-Duplication Rule

The IRS does not allow for a double deduction of wages for non-calendar year taxpayers:

Amounts that are treated as W-2 wages for a taxable year under any method cannot be treated as W-2 wages of any other taxable year. Also, an amount cannot be treated as W-2 wages by more than one trade or business.

VII. UBIA

A. General

The term qualified property means, with respect to any trade or business of an individual or RPE for a taxable year, tangible property of a character subject to the allowance for depreciation under section 167(a):

> (A) which is held by, and available for use in, the trade or business at the close of the taxable year,
>
> (B) which is used at any point during the taxable year in the trade or business's production of QBI, and
>
> (C) the depreciable period for which has not ended before the close of the individual's or RPE's taxable year.

Any improvements to qualified property are considered placed in service the year of the improvement. However, IRC 754 step ups are not considered new property and do not count towards qualified property.

For (C), depreciable period is not simply the MACRS period. Under 199A, the depreciable period is:

The period beginning on the date the property was first placed in service by the individual or RPE and ending on the later of:

> The date that is 10 years after such date, or
>
> The last day of the last full year in the applicable recovery period that would apply to the property under section 168(c), regardless of any application of section 168(g).

This allows for the qualified property to count, even if the taxpayer took bonus or IRC 179 depreciation in its original placed in service tax year.

B. Special Rules for Holding Periods

1. Property Held for a Short Period

Unless the taxpayer can show the purpose of acquiring the property was not for increasing the IRC 199A deduction, then ignore property that is:

1. Acquired within 60 days of the end of the tax year;

2. Disposed of within 120 days; and

3. Not used in the business for at least 45 days.

2. Like-Kind Exchanges and Involuntary Conversions

If the taxpayer has a like kind exchange or involuntary conversion, then the new property is considered replacement property.

For the 10 year rule, these assets will have a dual placed in service date. The dual placed in service date creates two sets of basis and placed in service dates to track:

1. The carryover basis from the asset the taxpayer gave up has a placed in service date of when the original asset was placed in service. Depreciation will continue based on the remaining life of the asset under the previous method used.

2. The excess basis over what basis was carried over has a placed in service date of when the new asset was acquired. Depreciation life and method will be new for this portion of the basis starting on the date of acquisition.

An election is available under Reg. 1.168(j)-6 to opt out of the dual placed in service date treatment above. The election allows a single combined basis under MACRS. This election treats the original asset as being disposed at the time of disposition and the new asset as having one basis and depreciation starts on the date of acquisition.

3. Tax Free Transactions

Tax free transactions include:

1. Complete liquidation of subsidiaries under IRC 332

2. Transfer to corporation controlled by transferor under IRC 351

3. Non-recognition of gain or loss on contribution to a partnership under IRC 361

4. Non-recognition of gain or loss on distribution to a partnership

5. Extent of recognition of gain or loss on distribution from a partnership under IRC 731; and

6. Transactions between members of the same affiliated groups, when that group files a consolidated return.

For these transactions, the assets acquired are considered placed in service as:

> For the portion of the transferee's unadjusted basis in the qualified property that does not exceed the transferor's unadjusted basis in such property, the date such portion was first placed in service by the transferee is the date on which the transferor first placed the qualified property in service; and

> For the portion of the transferee's unadjusted basis in the qualified property that exceeds the transferor's unadjusted basis in such property, such portion is treated as separate qualified property that the transferee first placed in service on the date of the transfer.

C. Unadjusted Basis

Generally, UBIA is calculated like any other asset. Just like normally determining basis for assets, UBIA does not include any personal use of the asset.

However, the following adjustments to basis are not included in UBIA:

1. Depreciation reduction under IRC 1016(a)(2) or (3)

2. Any basis adjustments due to tax credits claimed by the taxpayer

3. Any election to expense property under IRC 179, 179B, or 179C.

Example

On January 5, 2012, A purchases for $1 million and places in service Real Property X in A's trade or business. A's trade or business is not an SSTB. A's basis in Real Property X under section 1012 is $1 million. Real Property X is qualified property within the meaning of section 199A(b)(6). As of December 31, 2018, A's basis in Real Property X, as adjusted under section 1016(a)(2) for depreciation deductions under section 168(a), is $821,550.

For purposes of section 199A(b)(2)(B)(ii) and this section, A's UBIA of Real Property X is its $1 million cost basis under section 1012, regardless of any later depreciation deductions under section 168(a) and resulting basis adjustments under section 1016(a)(2).

D. Allocating Basis in a RPE

With an RPE, basis needs to be allocated to partners or shareholders according to the rules under Reg. 1.199A-2(a)(3).

The general rule is UBIA will be allocated to each partner or shareholder based on their share of depreciation.

1. Partnerships

In a partnership, for assets that do not produce tax depreciation for the year (i.e. property held less than 10 years, but whose recovery period has ended), each partner's share of the UBIA is based on how gain would be allocated to the partners pursuant to section 704(b) and (c) if the property were sold in a hypothetical transaction for cash equal to the fair market value of the qualified property.

2. S Corporations

In an S Corporation, for assets that do not produce tax depreciation during the year, each shareholder's share of UBIA is a share of the unadjusted basis proportionate to the ratio of shares in the S Corporation held by the shareholder over the total shares of the S Corporation.

VIII. SSTBs

As previously discussed, SSTBs follow a different calculation when calculating IRC 199A deductions. The test of whether or not a trade or business is an SSTB is at the business level, not the individual level. For example, a retired CPA is no longer doing accounting work but still gets a K-1 from his prior accounting firm. The SSTB rules apply to the business, not the individual, so the K-1 would be from an SSTB, even though the partner no longer performs accounting work.

The following are SSTBs:

A. Health

The performance of services in the field of health means the provision of medical services by individuals such as physicians, pharmacists, nurses, dentists, veterinarians, physical therapists, psychologists and other similar healthcare professionals performing services in their capacity as such who provide medical services directly to a patient (service recipient).

The performance of services in the field of health does not include the provision of services not directly related to a medical services field, even though the services provided may purportedly relate to the health of the service recipient.

For example, the performance of services in the field of health does not include the operation of health clubs or health spas that provide physical exercise or conditioning to their customers, payment processing, or the research, testing, and manufacture and/or sales of pharmaceuticals or medical devices.

B. Law

The performance of services in the field of law means the performance of services by individuals such as lawyers, paralegals, legal arbitrators, mediators, and similar professionals performing services in their capacity as such.

The performance of services in the field of law does not include the provision of services that do not require skills unique to the field of law, for example, the provision of services in the field of law does not include the provision of services by printers, delivery services, or stenography services.

C. Accounting

The performance of services in the field of accounting means the provision of services by individuals such as accountants, enrolled agents, return preparers, financial auditors, and similar professionals performing services in their capacity as such.

D. Actuarial Science

The performance of services in the field of actuarial science means the provision of services by individuals such as actuaries and similar professionals performing services in their capacity as such.

E. Performing Arts

The performance of services in the field of the performing arts means the performance of services by individuals who participate in the creation of performing arts, such as actors, singers, musicians, entertainers, directors, and similar professionals performing services in their capacity as such.

The performance of services in the field of performing arts does not include the provision of services that do not require skills unique to the creation of performing arts, such as the maintenance and operation of equipment or facilities for use in the performing arts.

Similarly, the performance of services in the field of the performing arts does not include the provision of services by persons who broadcast or otherwise disseminate video or audio of performing arts to the public.

Example

> A, a singer, records a song. A is paid a mechanical royalty when the song is licensed or streamed. A is also paid a performance royalty when the recorded song is played publicly. A is engaged in the performance of services in an SSTB in the field of performing arts within the meaning of paragraphs (b)(1)(v) and (b)(2)(vi). The royalties that A receives for the song are not eligible for a deduction under section 199A.

F. Consulting

The performance of services in the field of consulting means the provision of professional advice and counsel to clients to assist the client in achieving goals and solving problems. Consulting includes providing advice and counsel regarding advocacy with the intention of influencing decisions made by a government or governmental agency and all attempts to influence legislators and other government officials on behalf of a client by lobbyists and other similar professionals performing services in their capacity as such.

The performance of services in the field of consulting does not include the performance of services other than advice and counsel, such as sales or economically similar services or the provision of training and educational courses. For purposes of the preceding sentence, the determination of whether a person's services are sales or economically similar services will be based on all the facts and circumstances of that person's business.

Such facts and circumstances include, for example, the manner in which the taxpayer is compensated for the services provided.

Performance of services in the field of consulting does not include the performance of consulting services embedded in, or ancillary to, the sale of goods or performance of services on behalf of a trade or business that is otherwise not an SSTB (such as typical services provided by a building contractor) if there is no separate payment for the consulting services.

Example

C is in the business of providing services that assist unrelated entities in making their personnel structures more efficient. C studies its client's organization and structure and compares it to peers in its industry. C then makes recommendations and provides advice to its client regarding possible changes in the client's personnel structure, including the use of temporary workers. C is engaged in the performance of services in an SSTB in the field of consulting within the meaning of paragraphs (b)(1)(vi) and (b)(2)(vii).

Example

D is in the business of licensing software to customers. D discusses and evaluates the customer's software needs with the customer. The taxpayer advises the customer on the particular software products it licenses. D is Start Printed

Page 40926paid a flat price for the software license. After the customer licenses the software, D helps to implement the software. D is engaged in the trade or business of licensing software and not engaged in an SSTB in the field of consulting within the meaning of paragraphs (b)(1)(vi) and (b)(2)(vii).

G. Athletics

The performance of services in the field of athletics means the performance of services by individuals who participate in athletic competition such as athletes, coaches, and team managers in sports such as baseball, basketball, football, soccer, hockey, martial arts, boxing, bowling, tennis, golf, skiing, snowboarding, track and field, billiards, and racing. The performance of services in the field of athletics does not include the provision of services that do not require skills unique to athletic competition, such as the maintenance and operation of equipment or facilities for use in athletic events. Similarly, the performance of services in the field of athletics does not include the provision of services by persons who broadcast or otherwise disseminate video or audio of athletic events to the public.

Example

B is a partner in Partnership, which solely owns and operates a professional sports team. Partnership employs athletes and sells tickets to the public to attend games in which the sports team competes. Therefore, Partnership is engaged in the performance of services in an SSTB in the field of athletics within the meaning of paragraphs (b)(1)(vii) and (b)(2)(viii). B is a passive owner in Partnership and B does not provide any services with respect to Partnership or the sports team. However, because Partnership is engaged in an SSTB in the field of athletics, B's distributive share of the income, gain, loss, and deduction with respect to Partnership is not eligible for a deduction under section 199A.

H. Financial Services

The performance of services in the field of financial services means the provision of financial services to clients including managing wealth, advising clients with respect to finances, developing retirement plans, developing wealth transition plans, the provision of advisory and other similar services regarding valuations, mergers, acquisitions, dispositions, restructurings (including in title 11 or similar cases), and raising financial capital by underwriting, or acting as a client's agent in the issuance of securities and similar services.

This includes services provided by financial advisors, investment bankers, wealth planners, and retirement advisors and other similar professionals performing services in their capacity as such.

Example

> E is in the business of providing services to assist clients with their finances. E will study a particular client's financial situation, including, the client's present income, savings and investments, and anticipated future economic and financial needs. Based on this study, E will then assist the client in making decisions and plans regarding the client's financial activities. Such financial planning includes the design of a personal budget to assist the client in monitoring the client's financial situation, the adoption of investment strategies tailored to the client's needs, and other similar services. E is engaged in the performance of services in an SSTB in the field of financial services.

I. Brokerage Services

The performance of services in the field of brokerage services includes services in which a person arranges transactions between a buyer and a seller with respect to securities (as defined in section 475(c)(2)) for a commission or fee.

This includes services provided by stock brokers and other similar professionals, but does not include services provided by real estate agents and brokers, or insurance agents and brokers.

Example

>F is in the business of executing transactions for customers involving various types of securities or commodities generally traded through organized exchanges or other similar networks. Customers place orders with F to trade securities or commodities based on the taxpayer's recommendations. F's compensation for its services typically is based on completion of the trade orders. F is engaged in an SSTB in the field of brokerage services within the meaning of paragraphs (b)(1)(ix) and (b)(2)(x).

J. Investing and Investment Management

The performance of services that consist of investing and investment management refers to a trade or business involving the receipt of fees for providing investing, asset management, or investment management services, including providing advice with respect to buying and selling investments. The performance of services of investing and investment management does not include directly managing real property.

K. Trading

The performance of services that consist of trading means a trade or business of trading in securities (as defined in section 475(c)(2)), commodities (as defined in section 475(e)(2)), or partnership interests. Whether a person is a trader in securities, commodities, or partnership interests is determined by taking into account all relevant facts and circumstances, including the source and type of profit that is associated with engaging in the activity regardless of whether that person trades for the person's own account, for the account of others, or any combination thereof.

A taxpayer, such as a manufacturer or a farmer, who engages in hedging transactions as part of their trade or business of manufacturing or farming is not considered to be engaged in the trade or business of trading commodities.

L. Dealing in Securities

The performance of services that consist of dealing in securities (as defined in section 475(c)(2)) means regularly purchasing securities from and selling securities to customers in the ordinary course of a trade or business or regularly offering to enter into, assume, offset, assign, or otherwise terminate positions in securities with customers in the ordinary course of a trade or business.

For purposes of the preceding sentence, however, a taxpayer that regularly originates loans in the ordinary course of a trade or business of making loans but engages in no more than negligible sales of the loans is not dealing in securities for purposes of section 199A(d)(2) and this section. See § 1.475(c)-1(c)(2) and (4) for the definition of negligible sales.

M. Dealing in Commodities

The performance of services that consist of dealing in commodities (as defined in section 475(e)(2)) means regularly purchasing commodities from and selling commodities to customers in the ordinary course of a trade or business or regularly offering to enter into, assume, offset, assign, or otherwise terminate positions in commodities with customers in the ordinary course of a trade or business.

N. Dealing in Partnership Interests

The performance of services that consist of dealing in partnership interests means regularly purchasing partnership interests from and selling partnership interests to customers in the ordinary course of a trade or business or regularly offering to enter into, assume, offset, assign, or otherwise terminate positions in partnership interests with customers in the ordinary course of a trade or business.

O.   Any trade or business where the reputation or skill of the employees or owners is a principal asset.

The term any trade or business where the principal asset of such trade or business is the reputation or skill of one or more of its employees or owners means any trade or business that consists of any of the following (or any combination thereof):

(A)   A trade or business in which a person receives fees, compensation, or other income for endorsing products or services,

(B)   A trade or business in which a person licenses or receives fees, compensation or other income for the use of an individual's image, likeness, name, signature, voice, trademark, or any other symbols associated with the individual's identity,

(C)   Receiving fees, compensation, or other income for appearing at an event or on radio, television, or another media format.

(D)   For purposes of paragraph (A) through (C), the term fees, compensation, or other income includes the receipt of a partnership interest and the corresponding distributive share of income, deduction, gain or loss from the partnership, or the receipt of stock of an S corporation and the corresponding income, deduction, gain or loss from the S corporation stock.

Example

G owns 100% of Corp, an S corporation, which operates a bicycle sales and repair business. Corp has 8 employees, including G. Half of Corp's net income is generated from sales of new and used bicycles and related goods, such as helmets, and bicycle-related equipment. The other half of

Corp's net income is generated from bicycle repair services performed by G and Corp's other employees. Corp's assets consist of inventory, fixtures, bicycle repair equipment, and a leasehold on its retail location. Several of the employees and G have worked in the bicycle business for many years, and have acquired substantial skill and reputation in the field. Customers often consult with the employees on the best bicycle for purchase. G is in the business of sales and repairs of bicycles and is not engaged in an SSTB.

Example

H is a well-known chef and the sole owner of multiple restaurants each of which is owned in a disregarded entity. Due to H's skill and reputation as a chef, H receives an endorsement fee of $500,000 for the use of H's name on a line of cooking utensils and cookware. H is in the trade or business of being a chef and owning restaurants and such trade or business is not an SSTB. However, H is also in the trade or business of receiving endorsement income. H's trade or business consisting of the receipt of the endorsement fee for H's skill and/or reputation is an SSTB.

Example

J is a well-known actor. J entered into a partnership with Shoe Company, in which J contributed her likeness and the use of her name to the partnership in exchange for a 50% interest in the capital and profits of the partnership and a guaranteed payment. J's trade or business consisting of the receipt of the partnership interest and the corresponding distributive share with respect to the partnership interest for J's likeness and the use of her name is an SSTB.

P. De Minimis Rule

There are two de minimis rules that allow taxpayers a safe harbor allowing taxpayers to treat a trade or business as not an SSTB even though it has SSTB income.

These rules are:

1. When gross receipts are less than $25,000,000 during the taxable year, the trade or business is not an SSTB as long as gross receipts are less than 10 percent from an SSTB.

2. When gross receipts are more than $25,000,000 during the taxable year, if less than 5 percent of gross receipts are from an SSTB, then the trade or business will not be an SSTB.

Q.   Anti-Abuse Rules

To stop taxpayers from carving out SSTB income, the IRS proposed an anti-abuse rule.

An SSTB includes any trade or business that provides 80 percent or more of its property or services to an SSTB if there is 50 percent or more common ownership of the trades or businesses. Where 50 percent or more common ownership includes direct or indirect ownership by related parties within the meaning of sections 267(b) or 707(b).

Example

Law Firm is a partnership that provides legal services to clients, owns its own office building and employs its own administrative staff. Law Firm divides into three partnerships. Partnership 1 performs legal services to clients. Partnership 2 owns the office building and rents the entire building to Partnership 1. Partnership 3 employs the administrative staff and through a contract with Partnership 1 provides administrative services to Partnership 1 in exchange for fees. All three of the partnerships are owned by the same people (the original owners of Law Firm). Because there is 50% or more common ownership of each of the three partnerships, Partnership 2 provides substantially all of its property to Partnership 1, and Partnership 3 provides substantially all of its services to Partnership 1, Partnerships 1, 2, and 3 will be treated as one SSTB.

A second anti-abuse rules pertains to incidental to SSTBs:

If a trade or business (that would not otherwise be treated as an SSTB) has 50 percent or more common ownership with an SSTB, including related parties (within the meaning of sections 267(b) or 707(b)), and has shared expenses with the SSTB, including shared wage or overhead expenses, then such trade or business is treated as incidental to and, therefore, part of the SSTB if the gross receipts of the trade or business represents no more than 5 percent of the total combined gross receipts of the trade or business and the SSTB in a taxable year.

Example

A, a dermatologist, provides medical services to patients on a regular basis through Dermatology LLC, a disregarded entity owned by A. In addition to providing medical services, Dermatology LLC also sells skin care products to A's patients. The same employees and office space are used for the medical services and sale of skin care products. The gross receipts with respect to the skin care product sales do not exceed 5% of the gross receipts of Dermatology LLC. Accordingly, the sale of the skin care products is treated as incidental to A's SSTB of performing services in the field of health and is treated as part of such SSTB.

IX. Loss Carryovers

Whenever QBI is below $0, the 20% deduction is automatically $0 and you apply the carryover loss rules.

Take the total negative QBI and in the future year, treat the total negative QBI as a separate trade or business in the next tax year.

Qualified REIT dividends and qualified PTP income is grouped together for the purposes of these loss rules. So, if QBI is negative and Qualified REIT dividend and qualified PTP income are negative, then the carryover will be the QBI treated as a separate trade or business and the Qualified REIT divided and qualified PTP income carryovers which will offset such income in the future.

If the taxpayer is above the threshold amount, then the loss carryover rules are different. First, net QBI by apply a portion of the loss to each trade or business that has positive QBI. Then compute any applicable limitation.

Example

Person A had $100,000 of QBI and a $10,000 loss from qualified REIT dividends and qualified PTP income. The $10,000 loss does not offset QBI, but instead is carried forward to the next year and will offset any positive REIT dividends and qualified PTP income from that year.

X. Aggregation

Aggregation is a method of combining businesses for the purposes of IRC 199A. Aggregation is not necessary, however if a taxpayer is going to aggregate their businesses for the purposes of IRC 199A, then the taxpayer can only use the aggregation method proposed in Reg. 1.199A-4.

A. Aggregation - General Rule

In order to aggregate multiple trades or business, the taxpayer must:

1. The same person or group of persons, directly or indirectly, owns 50 percent or more of each trade or business to be aggregated, meaning in the case of such trades or businesses owned by an S corporation, 50 percent or more of the issued and

outstanding shares of the corporation, or, in the case of such trades or businesses owned by a partnership, 50 percent or more of the capital or profits in the partnership;

2. The ownership described in paragraph 1 exists for a majority of the taxable year in which the items attributable to each trade or business to be aggregated are included in income;

3. All of the items attributable to each trade or business to be aggregated are reported on returns with the same taxable year, not taking into account short taxable years;

4. None of the trades or businesses to be aggregated is a specified service trade or business (SSTB) as defined in § 1.199A-5; and

5. The trades or businesses to be aggregated satisfy at least two of the following factors (based on all of the facts and circumstances):

    (A) The trades or businesses provide products and services that are the same or customarily offered together.

    (B) The trades or businesses share facilities or share significant centralized business elements, such as personnel, accounting, legal, manufacturing, purchasing, human resources, or information technology resources.

    (C) The trades or businesses are operated in coordination with, or reliance upon, one or more of the businesses in the aggregated group (for example, supply chain interdependencies).

Example 1

A wholly owns and operates a catering business and a restaurant through separate disregarded entities. The catering business and the restaurant share centralized purchasing to obtain volume discounts and a centralized accounting office that performs all of the bookkeeping, tracks and issues statements on all of the receivables, and prepares the payroll for each business. A maintains a website and print advertising materials that reference both the catering business and the restaurant. A uses the restaurant kitchen to prepare food for the catering business. The catering business employs its own staff and owns equipment and trucks that are not used or associated with the restaurant.

A can aggregate these businesses.

Example 2

Assume the same facts as in Example 1 of this paragraph, but the catering and restaurant businesses are owned in separate partnerships and A, B, C, and D each own a 25% interest in the capital and profits of each of the two partnerships. A, B, C, and D are unrelated.

A, B, C, and D together own more than 50% of the capital and profits in each of the two partnerships, they may each treat the catering business and the restaurant as a single trade or business for purposes of applying § 1.199A-1(d).

Example 3

W owns a 75% interest in S1, an S corporation, and a 75% interest in the capital and profits of PRS, a partnership. S1 manufactures clothing and PRS is a retail pet food store. W manages S1 and PRS.

Although W manages both S1 and PRS, W is not able to satisfy the requirements of paragraph (b)(1)(v) as the two businesses do not provide goods or services that are the same or customarily offered together; there are no significant centralized business elements; and no facts indicate that the businesses are operated in coordination with, or reliance upon, one another. W must treat S1 and PRS as separate trades or businesses for purposes of applying § 1.199A-1(d).

Example 4

G owns 80% of the stock in S1, an S corporation and 80% of the capital and profits in LLC1 and LLC2, each of which is a partnership for Federal tax purposes. LLC1 manufactures and supplies all of the widgets sold by LLC2. LLC2 operates a retail store that sells LLC1's widgets. S1 owns the real property leased to LLC1 and LLC2 for use by the factory and retail store. The entities share common advertising and management.

G owns more than 50% of the stock of S1 and more than 50% of the capital and profits in LLC1 and LLC2 thus satisfying paragraph (b)(1)(i). LLC1, LLC2, and S1 share significant centralized business elements and are operated in coordination with, or in reliance upon, one or more of the businesses in the aggregated group. G can treat the business operations of LLC1 and LLC2 as a single trade or business for purposes of applying § 1.199A-1(d). S1 is eligible to be included in the aggregated group because it leases property to a trade or business within the aggregated trade or business as described in § 1.199A-1(b)(13) and meets the requirements of paragraph (b)(1).

Example 5

C owns a majority interest in a sailboat racing team and also owns an interest in PRS1 which operates a marina. PRS1 is a trade or business under section 162, but the sailboat racing team is not a trade or business within the meaning of section 162.

C has only one trade or business for purposes of section 199A and, therefore, cannot aggregate the interest in the racing team with PRS1 under paragraph (b)(1).

B. Attribution

When considering ownership for test 1, the IRS does allow for family attribution. Specifically:

1. The individual's spouse (other than a spouse who is legally separated from the individual under a decree of divorce or separate maintenance), and

2. The individual's children, grandchildren, and parents.

Example

G owns 80% of the stock in S1 and 20% of the capital and profits in each of LLC1 and LLC2. B, G's son, owns a majority interest in LLC2, and M, G's mother, owns a majority interest in LLC1. B does not own an interest in S1 or LLC1, and M does not own an interest in S1 or LLC2.

B and M's interest in LLC2 and LLC1, respectively, are attributable to G and G is treated as owning a majority interest in LLC2 and LLC. G may aggregate his interests in LLC1, LLC2, and S1 as a single trade or business for purposes of applying § 1.199A-1(d). S1 is eligible to be included in the aggregated group because it leases property to a trade or business within the aggregated trade or business as described in § 1.199A-1(b)(13) and meets the requirements of paragraph (b)(1) of this section.

Aggregation allows taxpayers to combine their share of QBI, W-2 wages and UBIA from the trades or businesses operated through RPEs. All three items must be aggregated if the taxpayer elects to aggregate the trades or businesses.

Once a taxpayer makes an aggregation election, the election is in effect for all future tax years. New businesses can be added to an already aggregated set of businesses.

If there is a change in facts and circumstances such that an individual's prior aggregation of trades or businesses no longer qualified for aggregation under the rules, then the trades or businesses will no longer be aggregated and the individual must reapply the aggregation rules to determine a new permissible aggregation, if any.

C. Election Statement

For each taxable year, individuals must attach a statement to their returns identifying each trade or business aggregated under the regulations. The statement must contain—

(A) A description of each trade or business;

(B) The name and EIN of each entity in which a trade or business is operated;

(C) Information identifying any trade or business that was formed, ceased operations, was acquired, or was disposed of during the taxable year; and

(D) Such other information as the Commissioner may require in forms, instructions, or other published guidance.

D. QBI Calculations with Aggregation

In order to get an idea of how the aggregation calculations work, we will start with an example where the taxpayer does not aggregate in order to see the differences compared to when the taxpayer does aggregate:

Example

F, an unmarried individual, owns as a sole proprietor 100 percent of three trades or businesses, Business X, Business Y, and Business Z. None of the businesses hold qualified property. F does not aggregate the trades or businesses under § 1.199A-4. For taxable year 2018, Business X generates $1 million of QBI and pays $500,000 of W-2 wages with respect to the business. Business Y also generates $1 million of QBI but pays no wages. Business Z generates $2,000 of QBI and pays $500,000 of W-2 wages with respect to the business. F also has $750,000 of wage income from employment with an unrelated company. After allowable deductions unrelated to the businesses, F's taxable income is $2,722,000.

Because F's taxable income is above the threshold amount, the QBI component of F's section 199A deduction is subject to the W-2 wage and UBIA of qualified property limitations. These limitations must be applied on a business-by-business basis. None of the businesses hold qualified property, therefore only the 50% of W-2 wage limitation must be calculated. Because QBI from each business is positive, F applies the limitation by determining the lesser of 20% of QBI and 50% of W-2 wages for each business. For Business X, the lesser of 20% of QBI ($1,000,000 × 20 percent = $200,000) and 50% of Business X's W-2 wages ($500,000 × 50% = $250,000) is $200,000. Business Y pays no W-2 wages. The lesser of 20% of Business Y's QBI ($1,000,000 × 20% = $200,000) and 50% of its W-2 wages (zero) is zero. For Business Z, the lesser of 20% of QBI ($2,000 × 20% = $400) and 50% of W-2 wages ($500,000 × 50% = $250,000) is $400.

Next, F must then combine the amounts determined in paragraph (ii) of this example and compare that sum to 20% of F's taxable income. The lesser of these two amounts equals F's section 199A deduction. The total of the combined amounts in paragraph (ii) is $200,400 ($200,000

+ 0 + 400). Twenty percent of F's taxable income is $544,400 ($2,722,000 × 20%). Thus, F's section 199A deduction for 2018 is $200,400.

Now, if the taxpayer does aggregate, the calculation is:

Example

Assume the same facts as in the example above, except that F aggregates Business X, Business Y, and Business Z under the rules of § 1.199A-4.

Because F's taxable income is above the threshold amount, the QBI component of F's section 199A deduction is subject to the W-2 wage and UBIA of qualified property limitations. Because the businesses are aggregated, these limitations are applied on an aggregated basis. None of the businesses holds qualified property, therefore only the W-2 wage limitation must be calculated. F applies the limitation by determining the lesser of 20% of the QBI from the aggregated businesses, which is $400,400 ($2,002,000 × 20%) and 50% of W-2 wages from the aggregated businesses, which is $500,000 ($1,000,000 × 50%). F's section 199A deduction is equal to the lesser of $400,400 and 20% of F's taxable income ($2,722,000 × 20% = $544,400). Thus, F's section 199A deduction for 2018 is $400,400.

The calculation is a little different if there are net losses. The first example looks at the calculation where the taxpayer does not aggregate and has net losses:

Example

Assume the same facts as in the first example, except that for taxable year 2018, Business Z generates a loss that results in ($600,000) of negative QBI and pays $500,000 of W-2 wages. After allowable deductions unrelated to the businesses, F's taxable income is $2,120,000. Because

Business Z had negative QBI, F must offset the positive QBI from Business X and Business Y with the negative QBI from Business Z in proportion to the relative amounts of positive QBI from Business X and Business Y. Because Business X and Business Y produced the same amount of positive QBI, the negative QBI from Business Z is apportioned equally among Business X and Business Y. Therefore, the adjusted QBI for each of Business X and Business Y is $700,000 ($1 million plus 50% of the negative QBI of $600,000). The adjusted QBI in Business Z is $0, because its negative QBI has been fully apportioned to Business X and Business Y.

Because F's taxable income is above the threshold amount, the QBI component of F's section 199A deduction is subject to the W-2 wage and UBIA of qualified property limitations. These limitations must be applied on a business-by-business basis. None of the businesses hold qualified property, therefore only the 50% of W-2 wage limitation must be calculated. For Business X, the lesser of 20% of QBI ($700,000 × 20% = $140,000) and 50% of W-2 wages ($500,000 × 50% = $250,000) is $140,000. Business Y pays no W-2 wages. The lesser of 20% of Business Y's QBI ($700,000 × 20% = $140,000) and 50% of its W-2 wages (zero) is zero.

F must combine the amounts determined in paragraph (ii) of this example and compare the sum to 20% of taxable income. F's section 199A deduction equals the lesser of these two amounts. The combined amount from paragraph (ii) of this example is $140,000 ($140,000 + $0) and 20% of F's taxable income is $424,000 ($2,120,000 × 20%). Thus, F's section 199A deduction for 2018 is $140,000. There is no carryover of any loss into the following taxable year for purposes of section 199A.

Here is the difference if the taxpayer aggregates the businesses:

Example

Assume the same facts as in the first example, except that F aggregates Business X, Business Y, and Business Z under the rules of § 1.199A-4.

Because F's taxable income is above the threshold amount, the QBI component of F's section 199A deduction is subject to the W-2 wage and UBIA of qualified property limitations. Because the businesses are aggregated, these limitations are applied on an aggregated basis. None of the businesses holds qualified property, therefore only the W-2 wage limitation must be calculated. F applies the limitation by determining the lesser of 20% of the QBI from the aggregated businesses ($1,400,000 × 20% = $280,000) Start Printed Page 40915and 50% of W-2 wages from the aggregated businesses ($1,000,000 × 50% = $500,000), or $280,000. F's section 199A deduction is equal to the lesser of $280,000 and 20% of F's taxable income ($2,120,000 × 20% = $424,000). Thus, F's section 199A deduction for 2018 is $280,000. There is no carryover of any loss into the following taxable year for purposes of section 199A.

XI. Miscellaneous Provisions

The following are a couple of random provisions that related to IRC 199A.

A.   Basis in Partnership or S Corporation

IRC 199A does not affect partnership or S Corporation basis.

B.   Self-Employment Taxes

IRC 199A does not reduce self-employment taxes.

C.   Net Investment Income Tax

IRC 199A does not affect net investment tax.

D. Alternative Minimum Tax

Do not adjust AMT for the IRC 199A deduction. No adjustments are needed to the IRC 199A deduction based on any AMT items that may be included in QBI.

E. Penalties

Substantial understatement penalties are assessed when the understatement of tax due exceeds the greater of $5,000 or 5% of the proper tax when the understatement relates to IRC 199A deduction.

F. RPE Reporting Requirements

All RPE's must report in Schedule K-1 each owner's allocable share of QBI, W-2 wages, and UBIA of qualified property attributable to each such trade or business and if the trade or business is an SSTB. Separately, the RPE must report any QBI, W-2 wages and UBIA in which the RPE owns a direct or indirect interest. It must also report the owner's share of qualified REIT dividends or qualified PTP income.

Failure to report this information means the amounts are presumed to be $0.

Appendix 1 – IRC 199A

(a) In general - In the case of a taxpayer other than a corporation, there shall be allowed as a deduction for any taxable year an amount equal to the sum of—
    (1) the lesser of—
        (A) the combined qualified business income amount of the taxpayer, or
        (B) an amount equal to 20 percent of the excess (if any) of—
            (i) the taxable income of the taxpayer for the taxable year, over
            (ii) the sum of any net capital gain (as defined in section 1(h)), plus the aggregate amount of the qualified cooperative dividends, of the taxpayer for the taxable year, plus
    (2) the lesser of—
        (A) 20 percent of the aggregate amount of the qualified cooperative dividends of the taxpayer for the taxable year, or
        (B) taxable income (reduced by the net capital gain (as so defined)) of the taxpayer for the taxable year.

The amount determined under the preceding sentence shall not exceed the taxable income (reduced by the net capital gain (as so defined)) of the taxpayer for the taxable year.

(b) Combined qualified business income amountFor purposes of this section—
    (1) In generalThe term "combined qualified business income amount" means, with respect to any taxable year, an amount equal to—
        (A) the sum of the amounts determined under paragraph (2) for each qualified trade or business carried on by the taxpayer, plus
        (B) 20 percent of the aggregate amount of the qualified REIT dividends and qualified publicly

traded partnership income of the taxpayer for the taxable year.

(2) Determination of deductible amount for each trade or businessThe amount determined under this paragraph with respect to any qualified trade or business is the lesser of—

    (A) 20 percent of the taxpayer's qualified business income with respect to the qualified trade or business, or

    (B) the greater of—

        (i) 50 percent of the W–2 wages with respect to the qualified trade or business, or

        (ii) the sum of 25 percent of the W–2 wages with respect to the qualified trade or business, plus 2.5 percent of the unadjusted basis immediately after acquisition of all qualified property.

(3) Modifications to limit based on taxable income

    (A) Exception from limit - In the case of any taxpayer whose taxable income for the taxable year does not exceed the threshold amount, paragraph (2) shall be applied without regard to subparagraph (B).

    (B) Phase-in of limit for certain taxpayers

        (i) In general - If—

            (I) the taxable income of a taxpayer for any taxable year exceeds the threshold amount, but does not exceed the sum of the threshold amount plus $50,000 ($100,000 in the case of a joint return), and

            (II) the amount determined under paragraph (2)(B) (determined without regard to this subparagraph) with respect to any qualified trade or business carried on by the taxpayer is less than the amount determined under paragraph (2)(A) with respect such trade or business,

then paragraph (2) shall be applied with respect to such trade or business without regard to subparagraph (B) thereof and by reducing the amount determined under subparagraph (A) thereof by the amount determined under clause (ii).

    (ii) Amount of reductionThe amount determined under this subparagraph is the amount which bears the same ratio to the excess amount as—

        (I) the amount by which the taxpayer's taxable income for the taxable year exceeds the threshold amount, bears to

        (II) $50,000 ($100,000 in the case of a joint return).

    (iii) Excess amountFor purposes of clause (ii), the excess amount is the excess of—

        (I) the amount determined under paragraph (2)(A) (determined without regard to this paragraph), over

        (II) the amount determined under paragraph (2)(B) (determined without regard to this paragraph).

(4) Wages, etc

    (A) In general 0 The term "W–2 wages" means, with respect to any person for any taxable year of such person, the amounts described in paragraphs (3) and (8) of section 6051(a) paid by such person with respect to employment of employees by such person during the calendar year ending during such taxable year.

    (B) Limitation to wages attributable to qualified business income - Such term shall not include any amount which is not properly allocable to qualified business income for purposes of subsection (c)(1).

    (C) Return requirement - Such term shall not include any amount which is not properly included in a return filed with the Social Security Administration on or before the 60th day after the due date (including extensions) for such return.

(5) Acquisitions, dispositions, and short taxable years -

The Secretary shall provide for the application of this subsection in cases of a short taxable year or where the taxpayer acquires, or disposes of, the major portion of a trade or business or the major portion of a separate unit of a trade or business during the taxable year.

(6) Qualified propertyFor purposes of this section:

    (A) In generalThe term "qualified property" means, with respect to any qualified trade or business for a taxable year, tangible property of a character subject to the allowance for depreciation under section 167—

        (i) which is held by, and available for use in, the qualified trade or business at the close of the taxable year,

        (ii) which is used at any point during the taxable year in the production of qualified business income, and

        (iii) the depreciable period for which has not ended before the close of the taxable year.

    (B) Depreciable periodThe term "depreciable period" means, with respect to qualified property of a taxpayer, the period beginning on the date the property was first placed in service by the taxpayer and ending on the later of—

        (i) the date that is 10 years after such date, or

        (ii) the last day of the last full year in the applicable recovery period that would apply to the property under section 168 (determined without regard to subsection (g) thereof).

(c) Qualified business incomeFor purposes of this section—

    (1) In general - The term "qualified business income" means, for any taxable year, the net amount of qualified items of income, gain, deduction, and loss with respect to any qualified trade or business of the taxpayer. Such term shall not include any qualified REIT dividends, qualified cooperative dividends, or qualified publicly traded partnership income.

(2) Carryover of losses - If the net amount of qualified income, gain, deduction, and loss with respect to qualified trades or businesses of the taxpayer for any taxable year is less than zero, such amount shall be treated as a loss from a qualified trade or business in the succeeding taxable year.

(3) Qualified items of income, gain, deduction, and lossFor purposes of this subsection—

(A) In generalThe term "qualified items of income, gain, deduction, and loss" means items of income, gain, deduction, and loss to the extent such items are—

(i) effectively connected with the conduct of a trade or business within the United States (within the meaning of section 864(c), determined by substituting "qualified trade or business (within the meaning of section 199A)" for"nonresident alien individual or a foreign corporation" or for "a foreign corporation" each place it appears), and

(ii) included or allowed in determining taxable income for the taxable year.

(B) ExceptionsThe following investment items shall not be taken into account as a qualified item of income, gain, deduction, or loss:

(i) Any item of short-term capital gain, short-term capital loss, long-term capital gain, or long-term capital loss.

(ii) Any dividend, income equivalent to a dividend, or payment in lieu of dividends described in section 954(c)(1)(G).

(iii) Any interest income other than interest income which is properly allocable to a trade or business.

(iv) Any item of gain or loss described in subparagraph (C) or (D) of section 954(c)(1) (applied by substituting "qualified trade or business" for "controlled foreign corporation").

(v) Any item of income, gain, deduction, or

loss taken into account under section 954(c)(1)(F) (determined without regard to clause (ii) thereof and other than items attributable to notional principal contracts entered into in transactions qualifying under section 1221(a)(7)).

(vi) Any amount received from an annuity which is not received in connection with the trade or business.

(vii) Any item of deduction or loss properly allocable to an amount described in any of the preceding clauses.

(4) Treatment of reasonable compensation and guaranteed paymentsQualified business income shall not include—

(A) reasonable compensation paid to the taxpayer by any qualified trade or business of the taxpayer for services rendered with respect to the trade or business,

(B) any guaranteed payment described in section 707(c) paid to a partner for services rendered with respect to the trade or business, and

(C) to the extent provided in regulations, any payment described in section 707(a) to a partner for services rendered with respect to the trade or business.

(d) Qualified trade or businessFor purposes of this section—

(1) In general - The term "qualified trade or business" means any trade or business other than—

(A) a specified service trade or business, or

(B) the trade or business of performing services as an employee.

(2) Specified service trade or businessThe term "specified service trade or business" means any trade or business—

(A) which is described in section 1202(e)(3)(A) (applied without regard to the words "engineering, architecture,") or which would be so described if the term "employees or owners" were substituted for "employees" therein, or

(B) which involves the performance of services that

consist of investing and investment management, trading, or dealing in securities (as defined in section 475(c)(2)), partnership interests, or commodities (as defined in section 475(e)(2)).

(3) Exception for specified service businesses based on taxpayer's income

(A) In generalIf, for any taxable year, the taxable income of any taxpayer is less than the sum of the threshold amount plus $50,000 ($100,000 in the case of a joint return), then—

(i) any specified service trade or business of the taxpayer shall not fail to be treated as a qualified trade or business due to paragraph (1)(A), but

(ii) only the applicable percentage of qualified items of income, gain, deduction, or loss, and the W–2 wages and the unadjusted basis immediately after acquisition of qualified property, of the taxpayer allocable to such specified service trade or business shall be taken into account in computing the qualified business income, W–2 wages, and the unadjusted basis immediately after acquisition of qualified property of the taxpayer for the taxable year for purposes of applying this section.

(B) Applicable percentageFor purposes of subparagraph (A), the term "applicable percentage" means, with respect to any taxable year, 100 percent reduced (not below zero) by the percentage equal to the ratio of—

(i) the taxable income of the taxpayer for the taxable year in excess of the threshold amount, bears to

(ii) $50,000 ($100,000 in the case of a joint return).

(e) Other DefinitionsFor purposes of this section—

(1) Taxable income - Taxable income shall be computed without regard to the deduction allowable under this

section.

(2) Threshold amount

(A) In general - The term "threshold amount" means $157,500 (200 percent of such amount in the case of a joint return).

(B) Inflation adjustmentIn the case of any taxable year beginning after 2018, the dollar amount in subparagraph (A) shall be increased by an amount equal to—

(i) such dollar amount, multiplied by

(ii) the cost-of-living adjustment determined under section 1(f)(3) for the calendar year in which the taxable year begins, determined by substituting "calendar year 2017" for "calendar year 2016" in subparagraph (A)(ii) thereof.

The amount of any increase under the preceding sentence shall be rounded as provided in section 1(f)(7).

(3) Qualified REIT dividendThe term "qualified REIT dividend" means any dividend from a real estate investment trust received during the taxable year which—

(A) is not a capital gaindividend, as defined in section 857(b)(3), and

(B) is not qualified dividend income, as defined in section 1(h)(11).

(4) Qualified cooperative dividendThe term "qualified cooperative dividend" means any patronage dividend (as defined in section 1388(a)), any per-unit retain allocation (as defined in section 1388(f)), and any qualified written notice of allocation (as defined in section 1388(c)), or any similar amount received from an organization described in subparagraph (B)(ii), which—

(A) is includible in gross income, and

(B) is received from—

(i) an organization or corporation described in section 501(c)(12) or 1381(a), or

(ii) an organization which is governed under this title by the rules applicable to cooperatives under this title before the enactment of subchapter T.

(5) Qualified publicly traded partnership incomeThe term "qualified publicly traded partnership income" means, with respect to any qualified trade or business of a taxpayer, the sum of—

 (A) the net amount of such taxpayer's allocable share of each qualified item of income, gain, deduction, and loss (as defined in subsection (c)(3) and determined after the application of subsection (c)(4)) from a publicly traded partnership (as defined in section 7704(a)) [1] which is not treated as a corporation under section 7704(c), plus

 (B) any gain recognized by such taxpayer upon disposition of its interest in such partnership to the extent such gain is treated as an amount realized from the sale or exchange of property other than a capital asset under section 751(a).

(f) Special rules

 (1) Application to partnerships and s corporations

  (A) In generalIn the case of a partnership or S corporation—

   (i) this section shall be applied at the partner or shareholder level,

   (ii) each partner or shareholder shall take into account such person's allocable share of each qualified item of income, gain, deduction, and loss, and

   (iii) each partner or shareholder shall be treated for purposes of subsection (b) as having W–2 wages and unadjusted basis immediately after acquisition of qualified property for the taxable year in an amount equal to such person's allocable share of the W–2 wages and the unadjusted basis immediately after acquisition of qualified property of the partnership or S corporation for the taxable year (as determined under regulations prescribed by the Secretary).

For purposes of clause (iii), a partner's or shareholder's allocable share of W–2 wages shall be determined in the same manner as the partner's or shareholder's allocable share of wage expenses. For purposes of such clause, partner's or shareholder's allocable share of the unadjusted basis immediately after acquisition of qualified property shall be determined in the same manner as the partner's or shareholder's allocable share of depreciation. For purposes of this subparagraph, in the case of an S corporation, an allocable share shall be the shareholder's pro rata share of an item.

    (B) Application to trusts and estates - Rules similar to the rules under section 199(d)(1)(B)(i) (as in effect on December 1, 2017) for the apportionment of W–2 wages shall apply to the apportionment of W–2 wages and the apportionment of unadjusted basis immediately after acquisition of qualified property under this section.

    (C) Treatment of trades or business in Puerto Rico

        (i) In general - In the case of any taxpayer with qualified business income from sources within the commonwealth of Puerto Rico, if all such income is taxable under section 1 for such taxable year, then for purposes of determining the qualified business income of such taxpayer for such taxable year, the term "United States" shall include the Commonwealth of Puerto Rico.

        (ii) Special rule for applying limit - In the case of any taxpayer described in clause (i), the determination of W–2 wages of such taxpayer with respect to any qualified trade or business conducted in Puerto Rico shall be made without regard to any exclusion under section 3401(a)(8) for remuneration paid for services in Puerto Rico.

(2) Coordination with minimum tax - For purposes of determining alternative minimum taxable income under section 55, qualified business income shall be determined without regard to any adjustments under sections 56 through 59.

(3) Deduction limited to income taxes - The deduction

under subsection (a) shall only be allowed for purposes of this chapter.

(4) Regulations The Secretary shall prescribe such regulations as are necessary to carry out the purposes of this section, including regulations—

    (A) for requiring or restricting the allocation of items and wages under this section and such reporting requirements as the Secretary determines appropriate, and

    (B) for the application of this section in the case of tiered entities.

(g) Deduction allowed to specified agricultural or horticultural cooperatives

    (1) In general In the case of any taxable year of a specified agricultural or horticultural cooperative beginning after December 31, 2017, there shall be allowed a deduction in an amount equal to the lesser of—

        (A) 20 percent of the excess (if any) of—

            (i) the gross income of a specified agricultural or horticultural cooperative, over

            (ii) the qualified cooperative dividends (as defined in subsection (e)(4)) paid during the taxable year for the taxable year, or

        (B) the greater of—

            (i) 50 percent of the W–2 wages of the cooperative with respect to its trade or business, or

            (ii) the sum of 25 percent of the W–2 wages of the cooperative with respect to its trade or business, plus 2.5 percent of the unadjusted basis immediately after acquisition of all qualified property of the cooperative.

(2) Limitation - The amount determined under paragraph (1) shall not exceed the taxable income of the specified agricultural or horticultural for the taxable year.

(3) Specified agricultural or horticultural cooperative For purposes of this subsection, the term "specified agricultural or horticultural cooperative" means an organization to which part I of subchapter T applies which is engaged in—

(A) the manufacturing, production, growth, or extraction in whole or significant part of any agricultural or horticultural product,
(B) the marketing of agricultural or horticultural products which its patrons have so manufactured, produced, grown, or extracted, or
(C) the provision of supplies, equipment, or services to farmers or to organizations described in subparagraph (A) or (B).

(h) Anti-abuse rulesThe Secretary shall—

(1) apply rules similar to the rules under section 179(d)(2) in order to prevent the manipulation of the depreciable period of qualified property using transactions between related parties, and

(2) prescribe rules for determining the unadjusted basis immediately after acquisition of qualified property acquired in like-kind exchanges or involuntary conversions.

(i) Termination - This section shall not apply to taxable years beginning after December 31, 2025

www.ingramcontent.com/pod-product-compliance
Lightning Source LLC
Chambersburg PA
CBHW071110240526
45469CB00006BD/2413